Music Genres

Hip-Hop

by Matt Lilley

FOCUS READERS
BEACON

www.focusreaders.com

Focus Readers is distributed by North Star Editions:
sales@northstareditions.com | 888-417-0195

Produced for Focus Readers by Red Line Editorial.

Photographs ©: Matt Sayles/Invision/AP Images, cover, 1; Shutterstock Images, 4, 8, 12, 20–21, 22, 25, 29; Steve Rapport/Hulton Archive/Getty Images, 7; Michael Caulfield Archive/WireImage/Getty Images, 11; Henry Iddon/PYMCA/Avalon/Hulton Archive/Getty Images, 14; David Corio/Michael Ochs Archives/Getty Images, 17; Raymond Boyd/Michael Ochs Archives/Getty Images, 19; Scott Dudelson/Coachella/Getty Images Entertainment/Getty Images, 26

Library of Congress Cataloging-in-Publication Data
Names: Lilley, Matt, author.
Title: Hip-hop / by Matt Lilley.
Description: Mendota Heights, MN: Focus Readers, 2025. | Series: Music genres | Includes index. | Audience: Grades 2-3
Identifiers: LCCN 2024001536 (print) | LCCN 2024001537 (ebook) | ISBN 9798889982005 (hardcover) | ISBN 9798889982562 (paperback) | ISBN 9798889983644 (pdf) | ISBN 9798889983125 (ebook)
Subjects: LCSH: Rap (Music)--History and criticism--Juvenile literature. | Hip-hop--Juvenile literature.
Classification: LCC ML3531 .L55 2025 (print) | LCC ML3531 (ebook)
LC record available at https://lccn.loc.gov/2024001536
LC ebook record available at https://lccn.loc.gov/2024001537

Printed in the United States of America
Mankato, MN
082024

About the Author

Matt Lilley has written more than 20 nonfiction children's books. He also has an MS in scientific and technical writing. The focus of his degree was on health writing for kids. He loves researching and writing about all sorts of topics. He lives in Minnesota with his family.

Table of Contents

Chapter 1

Beats and Rhymes

A **DJ** stands over a pair of **turntables**. The DJ moves one record back and forth. It makes a scratching sound. Then the DJ moves the other record. He keeps both records on the same **rhythm**.

Turntables are platforms that hold vinyl records. The turntables spin to make the records play.

The sounds mix together to make a new song.

Two **MCs** walk onto the stage. The crowd goes wild. Together, these three musicians make up a hip-hop group. They are Run-D.M.C. The two MCs start rapping. The rhythm of their words matches the song's beat. It is poetry set to music.

Did You Know?

Most hip-hop groups have at least one DJ and at least one MC.

Run-D.M.C. was the first hip-hop group with an album that sold more than one million copies.

The song ends. But the DJ keeps the beat going. The rappers move right into the next song. The crowd loves the show.

Chapter 2

What Is Hip-Hop?

Hip-hop comes from Black American **culture**. Hip-hop is about self-expression. Artists can use hip-hop to show where they came from. They might use it to explain their experiences.

Some people use expensive equipment to make hip-hop music. Others use simple tools at home.

Hip-hop music started with DJs. DJs played records on turntables. They played the records like instruments. DJs made new songs this way. Some musicians created complicated beats. People added different sounds over the beats.

MCs are another key part of hip-hop music. These artists write and perform rhyming lyrics. Their words fit with each song's beat and rhythm. Early MCs added simple chants. Over time, rap lyrics got

"Rapper's Delight" by the Sugarhill Gang was one of the first hip-hop songs to become famous.

more complex. Verses often use fast or detailed patterns of rhyme and rhythm. Lyrics cover many topics. Some lyrics focus on love or family.

Balance and flexibility are important for many breakdancing moves.

Success and overcoming struggles are other common topics.

Music is not the only part of hip-hop. Dance is important, too. Many hip-hop dancers move to a song's **break**. The style is called breakdancing. Graffiti is part of hip-hop culture, too. Graffiti is a visual art. Artists spray paint. They often sign their work. Clothing and attitude can also be part of hip-hop. Hip-hop musicians might use all these elements in their performances.

Did You Know?

Sometimes rappers make up lyrics on the spot. That is called freestyling. Rappers such as Busta Rhymes got their starts in freestyle rap battles.

CITY
5

Chapter 3

Hip-Hop History

Hip-hop was born in the Bronx in New York City. It started on August 11, 1973. On that day, DJ Kool Herc threw a party. He played music with turntables. But Herc didn't play full songs.

DJ Kool Herc is sometimes called the Father of Hip-Hop.

He just played the breaks. People loved dancing to them.

Herc's technique spread. DJs also invented new tricks. For example, Grand Wizzard Theodore came up with scratching. He moved records in a new way. Other artists learned those tricks and tried their own.

Early hip-hop songs used beats from other **genres**. Those included disco, funk, and soul. In the 1980s, groups started using drum machines. Then an artist called

Grandmaster Flash came up with many new DJ techniques. He performed with the Furious Five.

Marley Marl made an important discovery. He figured out how to **sample** bits of other songs. He recorded sounds. He could make changes or add parts. Other musicians started doing the same.

At first, many people thought hip-hop was a fad. They said it would not last. But in the 1980s and 1990s, Run-D.M.C. helped make hip-hop more popular. In 1984, the group released "Rock Box." It mixed hip-hop with rock music. New listeners became fans.

Did You Know?

James Brown was a soul musician. He became the most sampled artist of all time. Many hip-hop artists use parts of Brown's songs.

Tupac was one of the most famous rappers of the 1990s.

Over the years, hip-hop music spread further across the United States. In California, artists such as Ice-T and Dr. Dre made gangsta rap. In the South, OutKast and others created Southern rap.

ARTIST SPOTLIGHT

Lauryn Hill

Lauryn Hill was born in 1975 in New Jersey. Hill became an actress and a musician. She gained success in a hip-hop trio. It was called the Fugees.

In 1998, Hill released a **solo** album. In *The Miseducation of Lauryn Hill*, Hill mixed smooth singing with hip-hop. Listeners loved the album. It won many awards. The album helped hip-hop become popular with more people. And Hill's career inspired many female hip-hop artists.

Lauryn Hill was the first hip-hop artist to win Album of the Year at the Grammy Awards.

Chapter 4

Worldwide Hip-Hop

By the 2000s, hip-hop music was a standard part of popular radio. Many hip-hop artists were huge celebrities. Jay-Z was a global star. Eminem sold hundreds of millions of albums around the world.

By 2024, Jay-Z had won 24 Grammy Awards and 14 MTV Video Music Awards.

During the 2000s, the genre continued to change. Many artists mixed hip-hop with other genres. Fusions of hip-hop and R&B were popular. Rappers often worked with pop artists, too. Sometimes, artists mixed hip-hop with unexpected genres, such as country.

In the 2010s and 2020s, social media helped change hip-hop even more. Musicians could easily reach huge audiences. Lil Nas X put his song "Old Town Road" on

Travis Scott gained new fans by performing concerts in the video game *Fortnite*.

SoundCloud. In 2019, it became one of the most successful songs ever. Other artists such as Cardi B gained attention with Instagram. That helped Cardi get a record deal.

Sampa the Great combines traditional Zambian music with hip-hop.

Later, she won a Grammy Award for best rap album.

In the 2020s, hip-hop culture and hip-hop music continued to spread.

Now, many countries have their own hip-hop scenes. In England, artists grew a subgenre called grime. The Netherlands has "Netherhop." In Korea, K-hip-hop is popular. Hip-hop music started small. But now fans across the world love the genre.

Did You Know?

In 2017, Kendrick Lamar released his fourth album. It won the Pulitzer Prize for Music. It was the first hip-hop album to win this award.

FOCUS ON

Hip-Hop

Write your answers on a separate piece of paper.

1. Write a few sentences describing some common features of hip-hop.
2. Would you rather be a DJ or an MC? Why?
3. When did Run-D.M.C.'s "Rock Box" help hip-hop reach more listeners?
    - A. 1973
    - B. 1984
    - C. 2019
4. Who was the first hip-hop DJ?
    - A. Grandmaster Flash
    - B. Marley Marl
    - C. DJ Kool Herc

5. What does **complex** mean in this book?

*Over time, rap lyrics got more **complex**. Verses often use fast or detailed patterns of rhyme and rhythm.*

A. tricky or difficult

B. slow and boring

C. very simple

6. What does **fad** mean in this book?

*At first, many people thought hip-hop was a **fad**. They said it would not last.*

A. something that stays forever

B. something that goes away quickly

C. something that no one likes

Answer key on page 32.

Glossary

break

A part of a song that has a beat without lyrics.

culture

The arts and customs of a group of people.

DJ

An artist who plays recorded music. DJ stands for "disc jockey."

genres

Styles of music.

MCs

Rappers. MC stands for "master of ceremonies."

rhythm

In music, the mix of short and long sounds that create patterns.

sample

To take a short piece of music from one song and use it in another.

solo

Done alone rather than with a group.

turntables

Platforms that hold and turn music records.

To Learn More

BOOKS

Abdo, Kenny. *Rap Music History*. Minneapolis: Abdo Publishing, 2020.

London, Martha. *Lizzo*. Mendota Heights, MN: Focus Readers, 2020.

Smith, Elliott. *Black Achievements in Music*. Minneapolis: Lerner Publications, 2024.

NOTE TO EDUCATORS

Visit **www.focusreaders.com** to find lesson plans, activities, links, and other resources related to this title.

Index

Answer Key: 1. Answers will vary; **2.** Answers will vary; **3.** B; **4.** C; **5.** A; **6.** B